We Ask  a Blessing

❖

For Eileen,
with gratitude for the
blessing you have
been to me.
Love,
Ashley
June 2003

We Ask Your Blessing

100 Prayers for Campus Occasions

Donald G. Shockley

Writers Club Press
New York Lincoln Shanghai

We Ask Your Blessing
100 Prayers for Campus Occasions

All Rights Reserved © 2003 by Donald G. Shockley

Writers Club Press
an imprint of iUniverse, Inc.

For information address:
iUniverse
2021 Pine Lake Road, Suite 100
Lincoln, NE 68512
www.iuniverse.com

Cover photograph of candles in the All Faiths Chapel at Vanderbilt University is by Gerald Holly, 1993. Used by permission of Vanderbilt University.

ISBN: 0-595-26579-0

Printed in the United States of America

In Loving Memory of

Larry A. Green

Chaplain of Berry College in Rome, Georgia,

1972-1995

No matter what one believes in, there is something wonderful about blessing things.

Kathleen Norris, *Dakota*

Contents

Preface

About two years ago, a college chaplain used the Internet to raise a question with his peers concerning the prayers they provide at the annual commencement ceremonies. He felt that he was just repeating himself year after year and wondered how others approached the task. As a retired chaplain who gave public prayers on innumerable occasions during a long career in campus ministry, the question gave me an idea. Why not collect prayers from current religious leaders on American campuses and publish them as a resource? Utilizing two networks of college chaplains and campus ministers on the Internet, I shared the idea and asked any that were willing to do so to send me copies of some of their prayers. The idea evoked enthusiasm for the project and I began to receive prayers from chaplains and deans of religious life in colleges and universities from coast to coast. I was pleasantly surprised by the variety and quality of the prayers I received.

It is important for the reader to understand several things about the process that led to this book. Aside from the email invitation sent to the two lists of chaplains and campus ministers, no attempt was made to solicit additional prayers to achieve any sort of balance of representation. I simply added my own voluminous file of prayers to those I received and made choices from among them all. Some individuals sent one prayer while others sent as many as a dozen. I first sorted the prayers by the nature of the occasion for which each was prepared. Then I chose the prayers that seemed best to me in each of some fourteen categories. One consequence of this approach was that the competition was greater for some things, such as invocations at baccalaureate and commencement ceremonies, than for others, such as prayers at groundbreaking rituals and memorial services.

All of these prayers have actually been used on campus occasions as indicated, and I have left in elements that identify specific places and people (for example, the names of persons being inaugurated as college presidents, and of those for whom memorial events were held). It should also be said that, since nearly all of the colleges and universities that employ chaplains are private, though not necessarily church-related, all of the persons represented here work on private campuses. But the distinctions between public and private institutions of higher education are not nearly so great as one unfamiliar with the current scene might imagine. I will return to this point in the introduction that follows.

I here express my gratitude to the colleagues who have made this book possible by sharing their heartfelt sentiments and their gifts for expression in prayerful poetry as well as prose. The images they employ are unusually fresh and sometimes almost startling in their creativity and originality. The chaplains' passion for justice and peace shines through while at the same time their prayers often project a humorous dimension that is indispensable in communication with young people today. I encourage you to see the Contributors section at the end of the book to learn more about the authors of these prayers.

To whatever degree possible I have tried to maintain the distinctive forms employed in writing these prayers in advance of the occasions when they were read. The forms the prayers take are interesting in themselves and point to the care with which they were prepared. I personally grew up in a religious environment that equated spontaneity with authenticity; if you had to think about your prayers in advance you were not thought to be on good speaking terms with the Almighty. Ironically, public prayers produced in that manner tend to be unimaginative and quite predictable. One could not get away with that approach for very long on a contemporary campus and it is clear that none of the authors included in this collection would ever try it.

Almost all the chaplains and deans of religious life represented here are members of either, or both, of two professional associations: The Association for College and University Religious Affairs (ACURA); and the National

Association of College and University Chaplains (NACUC). Most of the participants in the former serve in private universities, while the latter primarily attracts chaplains of private liberal arts colleges. Both organizations, though small in membership, are very important to professional campus religious leaders. The relationships fostered among peers are not only professionally rewarding, but also vital to the collegiality that nourishes one's spirit in what is a unique and often undervalued role in higher education.

Many campus chaplains remember with great affection one person whose life among us was an incarnation of the very soul of our profession: Larry A. Green. After serving five years in campus ministry at Reinhardt College in Waleska, Georgia, he moved to Berry College in Rome, Georgia, where he served as chaplain from 1972 to 1995. During those years Larry was a devoted participant in and leader of NACUC. A person who was invariably radiant with delight, he was an inspiration to all who knew him, and certainly to his colleagues in ministry. This collection of campus prayers is gratefully dedicated to him as a sign that in spite of his untimely death we still remember and celebrate his life today.

Finally, as editor of this book, I express my appreciation to the Houghton Mifflin Company for permission to use a quotation from Kathleen Norris' *Dakota: A Spiritual Geography* as an epigraph. And I also thank Vanderbilt University for permission to use on the cover a photograph by Gerald Holley of candles glowing in the All Faiths Chapel on the Nashville, Tennessee campus.

Introduction

Even though the general triumph of secularism in higher education has worked against overt expressions of religious sentiment, the inclusion of prayers is still acknowledged as an important aspect of many public events and ceremonies in private colleges and universities. Graduation exercises are just the most obvious event to come to mind. But it also seems right to mark the beginning of a young person's college career as an important transition in his or her life. Then, too, when we celebrate Founders' Day, or when parents or alumni gather, or when special achievements are recognized at Honors Convocations, we need ceremonies to focus our feelings of gratitude and hope. And, unfortunately, there are those tragic moments when the death of a student, or some catastrophic event in the world, tears the fabric of community and calls us to gather in quest of restoration and healing. Always, there are public gatherings where we want someone to ask for the presence and blessing of God.

The secular spirit of higher education today is being challenged from what may seem like a surprising direction: the growing religious pluralism on American campuses. This is characteristic of the society as a whole of course, but in a campus setting where a diverse company of young people live in close relationships with each other day after day, religious issues are once more a pressing concern. Muslim students seek an appropriate place for Friday prayers, Hindu students apply for their own student organization, and so on. Interestingly, this attention to distinct religious traditions is occurring while, at the same time, more and more students who are unfamiliar with, or disaffected from, the institutional forms of faith have become spiritual seekers. The expression, "I am spiritual, but not religious," is routinely heard on campuses today.

Most of the private colleges and universities in America today were founded through the efforts of persons associated with Protestant forms of Christianity. Almost all of them have long since ceased to think of the churches that established them as their primary source for student recruitment, and their faculties as well as their student constituencies reflect to one degree or another the religious pluralism of contemporary America. Programs of religious life are continually changing to adapt to these new realities, as are traditional campus occasions such as baccalaureate services and commencement. Almost without exception, the prayers included here were offered in multi-faith settings. I well remember the time when, immediately before I was to offer an invocation at a fall convocation, the university president took me aside to say that, since the featured speaker for the day was Jewish, it would be especially important that I not conclude my prayer with the traditional "in Christ's name" ascription. I would not have done so anyway, but the president did not know that for sure since I was new to the place. It is a matter that has only become more important with each passing year.

In this space I will only mention the underlying theological challenge of prayer in multi-faith settings. For some religious leaders, to say a prayer in public that does not explicitly acknowledge their own faith tradition would be unthinkable. But it is the nature of prayers on communal occasions to be as inclusive as possible. For me to invoke a specifically Christian formula at the convocation mentioned above would have suggested to the speaker and others that when I said "we," they were not included. Some try to solve this problem by having several prayers offered by persons representing different religious traditions. That might have worked when it could be assumed that only Christians and Jews were present, but that is no longer a reasonable assumption. The tantalizing theological question here is whether or not there is any sense in which there is a spiritual kinship that, way down deep, unites us all as human beings regardless of our religious identities or lack thereof. I would answer the question affirmatively, and I think my colleagues would do so as well.

All of these concerns are evident in the prayers included in this book. A university chaplain now prays with sensitivity to the growing religious diversity of the campus as well as to the traditional presence of persons who feel that religion has no place in academia. And, we might add, a chaplain now prays with awareness of those who are highly motivated to have a spiritual life that is not dependent upon religious traditions and institutions, the new seekers. All of these prayers were actually offered on campus occasions by persons sharing a desire to ask for God's presence and blessing in an inclusive spirit. They can be a source of spiritual nourishment for individuals who read them privately. And they may serve as a guide for anyone, religious professional or not, who is called upon to offer a prayer in the context of a gathered, religiously pluralistic community.

I. Prayers At the Beginning of an Academic Year

1

O my soul,
what shall we say when our eyes flutter open
in the splendid clarity of early morning
and it's the first day of class
and we are more than ready but not yet ready?
> Be praised, O Great Mercy, for the awesome gift of life
> and for the courage we'll surely need for these days!

And what shall we say when we look about us
and perceive a realm of faces
for whom we do not yet have a name and story?
> Be praised, O Author of Grace, for the security of the steadfast among us,
> for the challenge and hope of new friends,
> and for the risk, chaos, and blessing of community.

And, O my soul, what shall we say when we lift our eyes to the hills
and our vision embraces stately yellow scaffolds
giving way to pale brick and sparkling window?
> Be praised, and Hallelujah-ed, O Creator,
> for your presence in the double edged gifts of history and progress,
> for promise and memory,
> and for carpets, cables, sidewalks and paint.

And so, O Eternal One, what shall we say?
     O Life!
     O Love!
     O Joy! Amen

Jan Fuller Carruthers

2

(based on a prayer by Rabbi Sheldon Marder)

New Trojans:
At this point of beginning,
we pause to summon strength,
to express gratitude,
and to invoke God's blessing.

This is a blessing about knowledge,
about those who want it, and yet are sometimes fearful of pursuing it.

This is a blessing about truth,
The hidden urge of the heart to know what is real and enduring.

This is a blessing about teachers and students—
the way they try hard to see the light,
to please one another and themselves.

This is a blessing about wisdom—
about how hard it is to find,
how hard as diamond stone to teach and to be taught,
to be learned and to learn.

This is a blessing about kindness,
about simple human caring—
how a good word, a smile, an opening outward,
can matter between people.

This is a blessing,
O, this is your blessing—
from me, from us, from the Eternal Spirit of the universe.
May you enter our gates in joyous expectation,
remain in strength,
and depart in celebration.

Go forward in peace,
go forward in blessing.
And let us say, Amen.

Rabbi Susan Laemmle

3

Eternal Wisdom,

Though the weather is not snowy, the wind not bitter,
        summer green has not even given way to autumn red and gold,

yet here we are—gathered for a New Year's party.

We have come together, despite an ominous humidity,
        to celebrate beginning again.

With pageantry, costume and song,
        with words for the soul and food for the body,
        we ring in this new year.

Let us know your presence among us in the smiling faces, clapping hands.

And as we enter this academic year of 2000-2001,

Draw your arms around those newly arrived
        that feeling homesick may soon be replaced by feeling at home;

Rekindle the sparks of curiosity and compassion in all those gathered here,
        and bless us with a renewing zeal;

that it may be said of Hobart and William Smith Colleges,

Indeed, Wisdom dwells with them. Amen.

Lesley Adams

4

Holy and Gracious God,

We are gathered today to officially begin our academic year. We thank you for the beauty of this day, and for the great variety in creation. We are bold now to ask your blessing on our year at Birmingham-Southern College, and for colleges and universities around the world. This is a day long anticipated by those of us who are beginning their college years. Bless their beginnings.

This is a day of honest ambiguity for those of us who have seen many beginnings and endings. Bless our history.

This is a day of painful sadness for those of us who grieve the losses experienced in our community. Bless their brokenness.

Holy and gracious God, we seek your blessing just as it was in the beginning, and is now, and ever shall be, world without end. Amen.

Stewart Jackson

5

Holy Wisdom, in whose many names we gather, be our teacher.

Teach us to seek you beyond and beneath all the knowledge we pursue. In a world flooded with information and parched for justice, guide our learning, our teaching, our living with courageous loving. Train us to see and embrace those we have been trained to overlook, those from whom our books may shield us: the outcast, the poor, the forgotten. Shape our hearts as surely as our minds around the common good, and help us to discover what is most good in all that is most common.

Holy Wisdom, be our teacher.

Teach us the wisdom of generosity—the simple kindness to make room in our lives for new friends, new colleagues, new students, new teachers; and give us the extravagant simplicity to know we need them as much as they need us. Make us perceptive enough to recognize the loneliness around or within us, strong enough to name it, and gentle enough to ease it. And grant us generosity of intellect—to inhabit our doubts long enough to befriend and follow them; to listen to those with whom we disagree long enough to learn from them.

Holy Wisdom, be our teacher.

Teach us the wisdom of humor and humility—the freedom to take ourselves lightly, to laugh, and the courage to live slowly and simply as though our worth did not finally depend on our work, because it doesn't. May we remember this year what this week we cannot forget: Life is brief, so let our kindness be swift and our perspective be broad.

Holy Wisdom, be planted deep within us and scattered wide among us, so that when the snows have come and thawed and the mud runs dry, and the daylight stretches again to its full length, we may be found at the far end of this new year flowering with humanity, mercy, friendship, and wisdom. Amen.

Kerry A. Maloney

6

O Lord, our Creator, we ask your blessing as we gather to mark the beginning of a new chapter in the life of our academic community. We remember with gratitude all whose efforts in years gone by have sustained this institution and passed on to us its good heritage and its broad horizon of opportunity. Give to this generation of teachers and students the simple joy of learning which brightens the spirit and welcomes the discipline of study.

While millions exhaust their strength in the basic struggle for physical survival and personal freedom, we would not be unmindful of the obligations which attend our good fortune. We are grateful for the presence among us of persons from other nations, and we pray that the opportunity for friendship with them will quicken our sense of membership in one wonderfully diverse human family.

Finally, we ask your blessing on all who are associated with Emory University in any way, and especially upon those who are now beginning their studies here. Amen.

Donald G. Shockley

7

Lord, if we could only be in two places at the same time! Here we are in this new place, asking questions we never thought about before: will someone eat dinner with me? Can three of us really live in a room this small? What will my classes be like? Is my major right for me? What *is* my major? Here we are, already forming friendships that will follow us forever, making choices that will change our lives, flirting with new, strange powers, touching new free-doms.

We also think of that other place, the place we have come from: home. It was a place we couldn't wait to leave, but have already begun to miss. The brother or sister anxious to possess our room. Parents who have long awaited this day when they could get rid of us, but are now struggling to say goodbye.

So now we entrust the anxieties and uncertainties of this moment to God, the greatest of all mysteries. We are praying that during the next four years our minds will be stretched, our spirits set free, and we will learn not only truth and knowledge, but also understanding and compassion.

"Grant us wisdom, grant us courage, for the living of these days." Go now and begin your new journey in God's peace. Amen.

Darrell Woomer

8

God of peace
and God of power,
you gave our founders a vision
of a place of learning
set amidst these green hills and valleys.

Yet, sometimes,
as we set out to seek the good, the true, the elegant,
as we work to stretch the sacred minds you gave us,

we fall back into comfortable roles
and the animosities among them.

In this new year,
grant us the freedom to forget our titles and our offices
when they no longer aid us in creating
the beloved community.

Grant us the breadth of spirit
to forget, sometimes,
the line between young and old,
owner and worker,
teacher and student,
to seek for all and for each
of our neighbors here
the greatest fulfilment of each and all,
in spirit, body, and mind. Amen.

Ian Oliver

9

We have been telling one another how sorry we are to leave summer's ease for school's rigors but Lord, we can also confess to excitement about the newness of this moment. Here we are, with new activities, new challenges, new friends, new joys. Surely you are in the midst of these. For all the gifts that come with this territory, we say thanks.

But we know, too, Lord, that this excitement will wither. The newness will become dull, like a much-used pencil. Days ahead will bring anxiety. Our joy will turn to worry. Time will be lost. The journey will grow long, and the tasks wearisome. Surely you will be with us in those days as well. Make your presence known to us through gifts that enable us to stay on course: wisdom, hope, patience, peace. When you give us a task, you also give us all we need to accomplish it.

Thanks for this moment; this semester; the past; the future; the Eternal Now, your home and ours. Amen.

William McDonald

II. Prayers at Luncheons, Dinners and Banquets

1

Table Grace (for Floyd and the housekeepers)

My friends,
what do we need in life?

Good food, lasting friendships,
the support of each other,
meaningful work,
a beautiful world,
strong loving families,
self respect and
the love of our God!

So, my friends,
what do we have to celebrate?

Good food, lasting friendships,
the support of each other,
meaningful work,
a beautiful world,
strong loving families,
self respect and
the love of our God!

All these things and more!
So let us eat together, and laugh.
Let us celebrate together, and live.
May God teach us to be grateful,
and so to be One.
In the name of our God,
Amen.

Jan Fuller Carruthers

2

At a Formal Dinner for New Students

Gracious God: It is you who willed us to be and to become in your image. It is you who imagined the wonderful potential of human life. It is you who breathed into our souls the need to ask why and for what purpose. Bless this group of students, some new to the privilege of higher education, others already engaged; this faculty, this staff and all who support and nurture this community as a place to become, to probe, to aspire. We thank you for this food, which reminds us of the abundance of life, and for all labor in any form that has brought it to us, for therein we are reminded of our debt to each other. Bless this gathering and bless this year, that it be fulfilling, challenging and happy. For we pray with gratefulness for all manifestations of your truth. Amen.

Don Fortenberry

3

At an Orientation Dinner

We thank you, O Lord, that you choose to speak to us in many ways. Let us receive this food as your Word to us, an expression of your loving concern for our lives.

Teach us, especially in these days, and in the weeks just ahead, how to listen for the sound of your voice; to realize that you may speak reassurance to us in the glance of a newly found friend. And help us to realize that, in our own kind word to a perfect stranger, you may send a signal of hope.

Most especially, dear God, prepare us for the days when we will be unable to hear your voice anywhere. As with a quiet moment in an intimate conversation, prepare us to receive the eloquence of silent spaces in our dialogue with life. In the name of One who laid down his life for his friends, Amen.

Donald G. Shockley

4

At a Holiday Dinner

In a world that seems to feed upon its own darkness, O Lord, we long to feast upon your true light. As the sun's bright rays have drawn this food from seeds planted in the earth, so may the light of your splendid face shine upon our souls and bring to the surface all that is good and holy in us.

In the festive seasons in which holy lights are kindled, we are especially grateful for the warmth and radiance that come from friendship. As we share food and fun, conversation and singing, we are reminded of just how blessed we are, and we are truly thankful. Amen.

Donald G. Shockley

5

Dinner Grace at the End of the First Year

We give thanks
for today and the relief of classes done
for the pride of success
for the learning of failure
and the hope of celebration.

We give thanks for these souls
for their gifts and loves,
for our bonds, challenges and wonders.

And we give thanks for
this food, these friends, the fun, the laughter,
and the chance to breathe.
We've survived!
Praise God! Hallelujah!
Sigh, O Wow! Amen.

Jan Fuller Carruthers

6

A Table Grace for Any Campus Meal

Blessed are you, Holy Sustainer, Nourisher of life
for bounteous gifts,
for banquets, picnics and festivals.

We take delight,
with all your holy ones,
in the bread and wine you create to share with us,
in the gift of laughter around tables,
for unselfish and generous giving
which sustains your purposes in this place.

Nourish us now, with each other's presence,
with the joy of loyalty and
the laughter of sharing.

Blessed are you, Lord our God,
who from our mother the earth
gives us daily bread to eat.

Jan Fuller Carruthers

III. Prayers for Honors and Awards Ceremonies

1

At An Honors Convocation

Our creator God, we bow before you today, invoking your blessing at this special time in the lives of these members of our university community whom we honor today. We thank you for the opportunities at the university to learn, to excel, and to lead. We praise you and offer thanks for the unique gifts you have bestowed upon the students we recognize today, the scholarship donors who have shared their gifts, the faculty and staff who have taught and given support and encouragement, and the family members and friends who have offered patience, support and love.

O wise God, we are grateful for the gift of the mind and the opportunity to pursue wisdom and knowledge. We give thanks and ask that your love and joy be instilled in us as we celebrate the achievements of those we honor today. Amen.

K. James Davis

2

At an Academic Honors Convocation

We begin with a Buddhist teaching: "Do not seek to follow in the footsteps of the heroes of old; instead, seek what they sought." This teaching offers perspective on today's occasion, when we come together to honor individuals who have achieved academic distinction. Surely each person who will be recognized today has drawn strength and inspiration from models of prior achievement. Every scientist works in the shadow of Newton and Einstein. For every artist, the past is both a burden and the template that encourages innovation. Each researcher stands alone at the cutting edge of knowledge and also upon the shoulders of those who have come before. It is natural and appropriate for us to look backward and sideward, measuring ourselves against what others, living and dead, have achieved. Seeing ourselves as part of a long, distinguished tradition brings humility but it also encourages us to make our best effort. The heroes of old and of our own time stand as beacons guiding us forward. Their accomplishments stretch the boundaries of what it means to be human, elevating us along with themselves.

And yet, we do well to repeat the teaching: "Do not seek to follow in the footsteps of the heroes of old; instead, seek what they sought." In the end, it is a vision of something beyond the human that truly inspires us. We reach towards something transcendent—towards truth, beauty, justice, perfection, and goodness. Keeping that elevated, transcendent goal clearly in mind saves us from small-mindedness and egotism. It set us on the road to largeness of spirit by enabling us to tap into universal wellsprings.

Thus, my voice speaks for those assembled here today, those being honored and those who gain inspiration from them, invoking blessings from the universal center to which all paths lead, toward which all true seeking sets its course. May the Eternal bless you and keep you. May the Eternal smile on you and favor you. May the Eternal smile upon you and give you—give us, give the entire world—Peace. And let us say, Amen.

Rabbi Susan Laemmle

3

At an Awards Luncheon

Times and seasons are yours, O God, and in your Providence you have appointed occasions for celebration and praise.

Be with us this day as with joy we gather to honor those who have been excellent stewards of the gifts you have given them. In honoring them, we give you thanks for the capacities of art, intellect, and industry, and for the exemplary manner in which the honorees have developed those faculties.

Hear our prayer of grateful praise for the gifts of friendship, food, and drink. Sustain us body, mind and spirit, that refreshed and renewed, we may ever bless and serve you by serving the little, the least and the lost of this world. And let your people say, Amen.

Mark Radecke

4

At An Honors Convocation

We gather this morning to honor
       those among us who are gifted
       with a sharp mind
       an agile body
       a keen eye
       a steady hand
       a soaring imagination
       a resolute will
       a gentle touch
       and an open heart.
We have come to honor
these Gifts of the Human Spirit

As we gather to honor
those who have been gifted
let us also honor our own giftedness
and remember to honor the Source of all
Good Gifts. AMEN

Bruce Coriell

5

Honors Day for Graduating Seniors

Creator God,

We thank you for these men and women who are completing their college years. Their families have launched them, this faculty has invested in them, and administrators have made them their prime concern. They are now ready to be graduated. Temper their knowledge with wisdom, their honors with humility, and their lives with service to humanity—on this day and all the days to come. Amen.

Stewart Jackson

6

At an Awards Banquet

Gracious God, on this special occasion we are reminded that, in the things that matter most in life, we are not alone. Countless people, many of whom are being recognized this evening, have shaped the contours of our lives and of our college community. The foresight and perseverance of the wise, the courage of the committed, the discontent of the perceptive, and the gentleness of the caring have blessed us. Individuals who care for justice more than comfort, truth more than acceptance and compassion more than convention have moved us. In our finest moments, we are blessed with individuals who remind us that all we are and all we have should finally serve a vision of human living filled with mercy, righteousness and truth.

We thank you for the privilege of being part of this community and for the satisfaction it has brought to our lives. Make us rightly grateful for all of life's blessings—food, health, community, faith and hope—which allow us to live with fullness and joy. Bless this occasion and use it to shape our desires and empower our souls. Amen.

Don Fortenberry

7

At A Black Awards Dinner

O Lord, our God,

Your servant Paul has reminded us that, if there is any excellence, if there is anything worthy of praise, we ought to think about such things. So we have gathered here in gratitude to recognize individuals whose achievements in this community are outstanding. Help us, as we honor the few, to be mindful also of the many who in countless ways have enriched our campus community and made our achievements possible. We give thanks for the noble men and women of former generations whose lives stand out as models of wisdom and courage. May we all be inspired by this occasion to follow more nearly their example. And as we serve in this university and in the world around us, help us hear your call to a still more excellent way. Amen.

Donald G. Shockley

IV. THE BLESSING OF BUILDINGS AND OTHER SPACES

1

A Physical Education Center

O Lord our Creator, we ask your blessing as we gather to dedicate the George W. Woodruff Physical Education Center. With deep gratitude to all whose efforts have brought us to this hour, we seek your guidance as we work to realize the full potential of this facility to serve the Emory community. May this magnificent structure renew in us our sense that the wholeness of life resides in the interdependence of body, mind and spirit. As this center becomes an active arena of individual achievement, may we also learn on its fields and courts the still greater joy of common effort. Amen.

Donald G. Shockley

2

A Campus Center

Loving God who calls us into community,

We give thanks for Wallace Alston for whom this campus center is named. May the students who use the center follow his example and be people of strength—in character, integrity, purpose, and faith. May this place be a hearth and home which nurtures the Agnes Scott College family, providing not only programming space, but also a heart for our life together. May its walls hear the laughter, music, and chat of happy times; the quiet, somber times of introspective search; and the lively debate of the free exchange of ideas. May the threads of different students' lives be woven in this loom into a glorious fabric of many colors and textures, that our community might continue to flourish in this century as it has in the last.

We pray trusting in your grace and power. Amen.

Laura S. Sugg

3

Two Prayers for the Opening of Libraries

Gracious God,

Today is a good day and we give you thanks.

We thank you for giving us this opportunity to celebrate, and we are grateful for those who have made this celebration possible. You have graciously endowed your servants with many gifts that have been used to make this rededicated building a reality.

For dreamers and builders and plumbers and architects,
we give you thanks.

For fund raisers and fund givers, for librarians and electricians,
we give you thanks.

For housekeepers and carpenters, carpet layers and trustees,
for citizens and students, administrators and teachers,
for book carriers, book borrowers, laborers and worriers,
we give you thanks.

For the gifts, for the gifted, and for the giver, we give our thanks and praise.
May this building be a place where minds young and old can come and be fed by the wisdom of the ages.
May it be a safe harbor for dreamers young and old to come and uncover the wisdom of the future.
May this building be dedicated to your glory and ourselves to your use. Amen.

Susan Olson

4

O Breath Eternal,
Your Word over chaos
shaped water, light, creature, flesh,
burst into blossom profusion,
diaphanous rainbow and song.
Be praised this day in thought, word, and deed,
in dream, sweat and gift.

Bless now, we pray, this house of learning
and all who labor in it
to teach, learn and love the true.
May it build unity instead of Babel,
humility over precedence,
and serve your will's progress
and never stumble.
We pray Your spirit hover over and within this library
as over all our houses,
so creating residences of life and laughter.

May all who here seek wisdom
be summoned by her favored face
to serve justice, speak truth, love adventure
until all our words,
printed, matrixed, danced and dreamed,
become our resounding holy Word—
first and last—
Alleluia. Amen.

Jan Fuller Carruthers

5

At the Opening of a New Chapel

O lord our God, we ask your blessing on this place, the William R. Cannon Chapel. May it be a sign for us of the renewal, in contemporary terms, of the vision that led to the founding of Emory University. Bless this place as an intersection for the human spirit expressed in so many cultures and faiths, by so many crafts and arts, by so many particular manifestations of the hopes and fears of all humankind. Let this house of worship realize its potential to accentuate the fundamental kinship of all persons.

Use this place, dear God, as a setting in which our minds are challenged by the whole truth, our spirits nourished by song and story and dance, and our wills fortified for whatever sacrifice justice may ask of us.

Finally, O gracious One, we ask you to surprise us by all this house of prayer and praise can mean for our campus and community. Although we are frail and proud creatures, in our heart of hearts we would will only that all our works be done for the glory of your holy name. Amen.

Donald G. Shockley

6

At the Dedication of a University Center

O God, our Creator, we thank you for this beautiful day, and for the foretaste of springtime which it brings. Our spirits are twice brightened today, for we have gathered to celebrate a most welcome event, long awaited. We ask your blessing as we dedicate the R. Howard Dobbs University Center.

Once again, we give you thanks for Emory University, for both its heritage and its hopes. On this occasion we offer special thanksgiving for all whose gifts, whose creative imaginations, whose diligent planning and hard work have brought us to this hour. Dear God, give your blessing to this marvelous building, so wonderfully blending the old and the new. By your grace may it draw us together more closely than ever before as one community bound by purposes which are noble and strong.

Most especially today, we give you thanks for the present generation of Emory students, and pray that all who serve them in this place may do so with wisdom, grace and strength. Amen.

Donald G. Shockley

V. Prayers for Baccalaureate Services

1

God, who beckons us forward in the march of life, we honor those who have enlisted themselves in the pursuit of the good.

Especially, we admire those who will receive degrees tomorrow,
noting their fervent patience in striding toward their dreams,
their surrendering of pride to invite knowledge in,
and their desire to be stewards of the treasures they have inherited:
treasures of talent that are a birthright, passed on from parent to child,
and treasures that are in surrounding resources whispering for attention and use.

May we step in line with these students-soon-to-be-called-graduates
and continue to consider your work and word in all that we do, all that we are,
and all that is of this world...

Ashley Cook

2

A sage of the 5th century posited that God may be a holy sphere, "whose center is everywhere; whose circumference, nowhere."

Here, in this particular arc of that divine sphere, among family members and friends, mentors and colleagues, teachers and students, and honored guests, let us pause together on this breath-taking occasion to catch our breath and be caught by the breath, the wind of the holy, which is to pray:

O Immensity of Love, Eternity of Mercy, in whose many names we gather,
bless to us the spirit of this magnificent sphere which we always inhabit but scarcely know;
the spirit of celebration and the freedom to revel in these glorious days of accomplishment;
the spirit of wisdom and the personal integrity to continue in its pursuit;
the spirit of humility and the dignity to cultivate; the spirit of justice and the courage to fashion it.

In this circle, marvelous in the diversity of its members, on this day, intricate in the complexity of its hopes, may we be so drawn to the center of the Holy Sphere that we will long to dwell there forever, in your heart, Love Immense, Mercy Eternal. Amen.

Kerry A. Maloney

3

The stars of heaven,
awesome in their majesty,
are not more wonderful
than the One who charts their course.

The elements
arrayed in perfection,
are not marvels greater
than the mind that beholds them.

This miracle, matter,
begets a wonder:
the body thinks,
insight comes from flesh;
the soul is born of dust
to build towers of hope,
opening within us
doors of lamentation and love.
For You have made us little less than divine,
and crowned us with glory and honor!

You, spirit of the universe, have blessed us with bodies, minds, and souls that strive for fulfillment and for love. Help us to achieve our promise and accept our limitations. Help us to join with others in the pursuit of common goals that are worthy of your blessing. In partnership with you, help us surely, even if slowly, to repair our broken but very beautiful world. Be with our graduates as they create their lives and do your work.

And let us all say, Amen.

Rabbi Susan Laemmle

4

Gracious God, as we assemble on this very special occasion, we are grateful indeed for the gift of life, that precious commodity in which we construct meaning and envision the future. We come together in this sacred place to acknowledge that all that makes us humane in mind, soul and spirit emanates from the reality we encounter in you. As we look out on these splendid students, we are reminded of the rare gift of having been part of their lives during this crucial time in their history.

We have been privileged to share their dreams and their triumphs, their pain, sadness—even their sorrows—and finally, their joys. We are grateful for the relationships that have developed and we anticipate the unfolding richness that will come as we, with pleasure and satisfaction watch their lives unfold over the years. Sanctify this time together to remind us in our deepest wells of meaning that our pilgrimage as human beings is finally and fundamentally one of the spirit, so that we not misplace our hope, and misuse our potential. For we pray in Christ's name. Amen.

Don Fortenberry

5

Transforming God, open our hearts to hear the still, small voice which sounds like silence to our straining ears. Teach us to know you for what you really are:

love :
flowing like a fountain,
steady as a mountain,
present in friendships and communities
constant in stillness and solitude.

Worker of great wonders, We praise you for what has been, for that which is today and for all that is yet to be. We thank you for what you have woven from the lives that meet here at The College of Wooster. For the futures which come into being out of slivers of love,

bits of trust,
snippets of hope,
rainbows of laughter , tears,
and worship

that out of the songs and struggles, failures and triumphs of this place and others like it, you have written on the hearts of a people who will carry the future of our world forward.

We praise you for the opportunity to stand on the edge between now and perhaps. Welcoming the new and accepting our limits, we look forward to so many possibilities. Transform us and our world.

Soften our experiences into wisdom. Turn our intelligence into justice. Translate our passion into action.

As we explore possibilities, may we choose wisely, live justly and act with reverence and compassion for our world and for all of life.

Help each of us to believe in transformation: for ourselves and for others;
for our close companions and those we contend with;
for those we love intimately and for strangers whose faces we only imagine;
for humans, for crawlers, swimmers and soarers, for plants, rocks, sea and air.

Be present in all our futures, for we know that with you, all things are possible.
Amen.

Linda Morgan-Clement

6

Creator God, in your wisdom you have formed us and by your wisdom you sustain our lives and this wondrous world. Give us joy in your creation and in our lives together.

You keep covenant with your people and summon us to lives of faithfulness and service. Bind these virtues around our necks and write them on the tablets of our hearts.

Free our tongues and fire our imaginations. Visit the members of the Class of 2001 with creativity, and send them out to the workplace, to graduate and professional schools, to home and family, to the community and the world as salt and leaven and light.

God of the future, so much more than God of the past, by your Spirit, enlarge our spirits. Make us people of hope, patient to wait, eager to respond.

These things we ask in your name, and let your people say *Amen!*

Mark Radecke

7

Invocation: to call upon

We honor creator,
        spinner of the web.

We greet ancestor,
        carrier of wisdom.

We invite muse,
        voice of inspiration.

We welcome guide,
        companion on the way,

and always we invoke spirit,
        giver of gifts, sender of dreams,
        healer of wounds, lover of life

We call upon your presence.

Bruce Coriell

8

O God, as we began this academic year with prayers, so also we end it: turning aside from our busy lives to ask your blessing on this hour. Let these moments have special significance for each one of us, renewing our spirits and bringing fresh focus to our hopes.

On this annual occasion in the life of our university, we remember before You those of our number who have died during the year. The memory of them is dear to us, and once more we express our gratitude for the many ways in which they served our common life, both in the tasks they performed and in the personal relationships we shared with them. Be always near their families and close associates that they may continuously find in your presence strength and courage adequate to their needs.

Most especially today, we ask your blessing upon these, our students, who are completing their undergraduate years. So guide the thoughts of all of us in this time of worship and reflection that we may once more experience those attitudes of mind and spirit that represent the best that is in us. And send us to our individual futures prepared to be loyal citizens of the age that is yet to be, when Your will shall be done on earth, even as it is in heaven. Amen.

Donald G. Shockley

VI. INVOCATIONS AT COMMENCEMENT CEREMONIES

1

Sing to the Holy One a new song!
Make a joyful noise;
Break forth into joyous song and sing praises!
With trumpets and the sound of the horn
Make a joyful noise! (from Psalm 98)

Author of Wisdom, you have led us here this morning to celebrate!
Our hearts are full of thanksgiving:

> for parents who have paid bills, listened to sobbing phone calls or gone without much communication at all for four years;

> for professors and coaches who have encouraged and cajoled the classes of '99 to do and to be their best;

> for clerical staff and administrators who taught them the importance of making good choices and the consequences of making poor ones;

> for the folk in food service, security, housekeeping, buildings and grounds, and for the trustees who have seen to it that they had food and safety and a beautiful place in which to live.

But our hearts are also full of sadness:

> for an era ended;
> for things left undone;
> for friends about to part company.

Bless our speakers with your wisdom, that they may touch our sorrow even as they stir us to new ventures.

And now enliven our hearts with joy,
draw our minds from wandering,
and help us be fully present with you and with one another,
that we might know you in the applause and shouts and whistles
that will send these graduates on their way. Amen.

Lesley Adams

2

God, whose height surpasses our imagination,
and whose depth reaches far beneath our consciousness,
today is a monument to wisdom,
each course taken a brick in the infinite tower of learning,
carefully coaxed into place by faculty and staff,
secured with the curious mortar of students striving to come into their own,
seeking to serve the human community by honoring the resources you have
bestowed in their hearts, minds, bodies, and souls.

We gather to express our awe at this collective accomplishment,
stretching our shoulders backward and turning our eyes upward to envision
all that is yet to be built, even as we marvel at what has been constructed thus
far.

Move this moment beyond a tiny turret of achievement into an expansive
sanctuary of security where spirits are invigorated with courage for the climb
of life.

May each name etched into this list of graduates inspire us all to pursue our
potential, to approach the world with wonder, and to delight in the knowledge
you have bequeathed to us to cherish and share. Amen.

Ashley Cook

3

We thank you, God of all ages and places,
For this place,
And its almost quaint idea
Of a place where the young gather,
Where truth is sought, found, and perhaps shared.

For the glorious passing of the years
That has seen these fledglings gain their plumage
While we, their elders, have watched ours thin and grey.

For those moments in this journey
When, in the daily pursuit of grades, love, and paychecks,
We happened upon truth,
And truth that left us stunned
By its awful beauty and power.

For the times we were lifted up
And carried outside ourselves
To see the depth of human misery in a stranger's face
And the undeserved privilege we have forgotten to remember.

For a day of funny hats and medieval ritual,
When we commit ourselves again
To the human struggle for that ultimate, peaceful, pure truth,
Unnamed and unnamable

For our time here on this hill,
Overlooking the river,
Where we have had a taste
Of the joys of discovery
And the companionship of kindred souls. Amen.

Ian Oliver

4

Giver of all wisdom,

You are the artist whose masterpieces of magnolia, mountain laurel and mockingbird song surround us each day. You are the scientist who knows the measure of a molecule and choreographs the movement of galaxies. You are the Word, gifting us with the power to speak and write—however haltingly—about the majesty of creation, the power of redemption, and the tenderness of affection.

You are the light that overcomes the darkness. You are the truth that sets us free. Illumine the paths of our graduates and our paths, that we may seek the way of compassion more than competition, of justice more than just desserts, of liberation more than appropriation.

Grant on this important day that we might recognize your presence with us, and that our thirst for truth amidst a free exchange of ideas might not end with graduation, but follow us into all the world.

Give our graduates the ability to look beyond the tensions of moving, of change, of family differences to see the gift you give us in our families and friends. And grant us the courage to speak a word of love and gratitude to people with whom we may find it difficult to express our feelings.

We pray for loved ones who could not be here today, and for people known and unknown to us who need the touch of a caring person.

I pray that each of us, especially our graduating seniors, might chart a course which leads closer to you and which contributes to our neighbor and our world. Amen.

Laura S. Sugg

5

Oh Divine Promise,
joy and bless
in proud amazement
the minds, hearts, souls and bodies
gathered beneath sunlit hills and crystal sky.

Holy Moment,
make stable and memorize
the fullness of this present love
to lifted, sparkling and wetted eyes.

Transcendent Hope,
be for us the laughter and tears
of futures yet discovered, grappled,
and embraced until
every ending bears creation's beginning
and until Your glory may be seen
in holding on and in letting go.

God's great name be praised. Amen.

Jan Fuller Carruthers

6

The sacred lesson envelops us

the warm embrace of sunshine
the raw power of wind
the fresh vitality of rain
the majestic display of lightning
the random dance of hail
the delicate wildness of snow
the piercing grip of cold
the warm embrace of sunshine

within hours we experience it all
   to live in any single moment
   alone would be our end,
only combined do we thrive
   within our world

and yet here we gather as different
from one another as night from day
the many hued colors
   and the textures of our skin
the surprising array of who we
   love and with whom we live
the numerous ways we
   experience the strengths and
   frailties of our bodies

the various places whence we
    come and to where we go
the different values which
    excite our passions and
    receive our commitments

we are exquisite in our diversity

and yet here we gather as connected
to each other as the night to the day

dare I call us a community
    children of the universe
    offspring of the spirit

unique individuals
common humanity
    progeny of the divine

Bruce Coriell

7

Come, let us sing to the Holy One
  let us shout for joy to the Rock of our salvation
Let us come before the presence of Holiness with thanksgiving,
  and raise a loud shout to God with praise. (from Psalm 95)

Giver of every good gift,
You have brought us to this day of celebration,
  sparking the creativity and caring of our faculty
  in classrooms, labs, offices,
  and even in committee meetings.

You have kindled dedication in those who have guided these graduates
  on playing fields and in residences,
  through crises and innumerable drop/adds.

You have ignited the passionate support of parents and trustees,
  grounds crews and housekeeping staffs,
  security and friends.

And we know that You have been with the classes of 2000
  from candle lighting on the quad to the senior toast at Houghton
  from finding courses first year, to selecting majors,
  from early morning classes to late nights in Gulick
  (and even later nights with friends.)

Help us to know your presence on this festive morning.
Inspire us to listen for Your wisdom in the words of our speakers,
    to give thanks to You as we applaud the graduates,
    and to praise Your many names as we shout for joy
    (in all weathers!) Amen.

Lesley Adams

8

Our creator God, author of knowledge, source of wisdom and truth, sacred presence with us today for this truly celebrative occasion, we have gathered to honor those who graduate this day from the University of Puget Sound. We join in the vision of our university's founders and all those who, for the past 109 years, have gathered as do we today to recognize and honor those who have completed the requirements for graduation.

We ask that you hear our prayer as we offer our deep and heartfelt thanks:

> For the students who today attain an important goal and embark upon new beginnings, opportunities, and challenges. May they take their skills, talents, visions and dreams to a world hungry for justice and hope.

> For the faculty and staff members, whose commitment to teaching has challenged their students to excel.

> For the families and friends, whose support and encouragement were vital in the pursuit of this academic degree.

Bless us all with the determination to be persons of integrity and compassion, and to possess a desire for truthfulness and justice. With trust in you and with hope and great thanksgiving we offer our prayer.

In the words of the Salish, first people of this land, we say *Kloshe Kawkwa*! So be it! Amen.

K. James Davis

9

O Holy One,

Sacred source of all that is good and beautiful and excellent,

We ask your Presence with us as we affirm the lives and the
achievements of those whom we have gathered here to honor.

Help us to remember with humility the many gifts we have been given,
and the heavy obligations that our privilege demands of us.

As we praise works that have been so impressively completed,
help us to remember those whose very lives depend on the quality of our
labor, the generosity of our spirits and the preservation of our common world.

As we sit together in peace and bounty, let us remember those for
whom peace and bounty are only a hope or a wish.

Be with these graduates, these precious children, our brothers and sisters, our
husbands and wives and family members and friends as they move through
these most promising and daunting days of transition. May their journey into
the next calling of their lives be blessed with success and creativity and the
security that only deep connections to other human beings and the earth itself
can offer.

Help them to focus radically on those truths they hold most deeply, to enact those truths in their work and in their lives, and may we all be given the gift of gratitude as we go from this place.

Be with us now as we celebrate. Amen.

Gay Welch

10

Our gracious God,

Thank you for this glorious day of celebration for the graduates. We are grateful for their families, friends, teachers, and a host of others who helped them complete the degrees they receive from Mary Baldwin College today. We send them forth with pride and affection, and we ask that you add your blessing upon them to ours. We cannot ask that they never have problems—that isn't the nature of life—but we do ask that you protect them from being led into situations that would destroy them.

> When they encounter life's challenges, give them your wisdom.
> When life brings them sorrow, you give them joy.
> Give them work to do, something you need to have done and they are good at.
> When they have success, give them the gift of graciousness toward others.
> If they are tempted to become cynical and discouraged, and to give up on the world,
> You be there to draw them into love of life all over again.
> Wherever they go, find them fit companions when they are lonely.

Teach us all, O God, to live with compassion and fairness; for the world needs both. May grandeur and generosity of spirit so characterize our lives that your image will shine through us. Amen.

Patricia Hunt

VII. Prayers at Memorial Services and Events

1

Dedication of a Memorial Bench

Gracious God, you have given us this wondrous good earth, so full of life in all its multiple forms: life in the seas, in the air, on the land. And you have given to the human family the responsibility of being good stewards of all this variety, this astonishing abundance.

Some of us, like Fred Feudale, are especially drawn to this life of stewardship. Some of us, like Fred, show a deep reverence and love for plant life, for its strength expressed in these oak trees, for the fragrance we receive from these magnolias, for the abundance of colors in the flowers of each season.

We thank you for our friend Fred who never tired of his work at Elon University, whose work gave him joy, and whose work kept him in touch with so many friends in all areas of Elon's community. We have felt the grace of your presence in our friendships with Fred.

We pray that his legacy of loving Elon's beauty and caring for it personally will remain strong in the daily practices of each of us. And we pray that his family will be strengthened by seeing today that Fred is still knitting us together in bonds of friendship.

Finally, O God, we pledge our commitment to seeing that at Elon, the beauty of the campus itself will serve to nourish our spirits. For we are in the business here of enhancing all forms of intelligence, the life of the mind, yes, but also the life of the soul. And our souls are fed, as Fred well knew, when we pause before a well kept flowerbed, when we admire the majesty of trees and the resilience of grass.

For the witness of our friend and colleague Fred Feudale that life and work can be joyously combined to nourish our souls, we give you thanks. In your name we pray. Amen.

Richard McBride

2

Planting A Tree In Memory of A Student

Then God said, "Let the earth put forth vegetation; plants yielding seed, and fruit trees of every kind on earth that bear fruit with the seed in it"; and it was so. The earth brought forth vegetation: plant yielding seed of every kind, and trees of every kind bearing fruit with the seed in it. And God saw that it was good. (Genesis 1:11-12)

Gracious God,
We thank you for the rhythm of life you have created. We thank you that you have called everything in creation good. Today we bless in your name this tree and the life it reminds us of. May it grow, give shade and oxygen to us all, and may we all remember that life it will forever symbolize. In your gracious name we pray. Amen.

Stewart Jackson

3

At A Holocaust Remembrance Service

Blessed art Thou O Lord our G-d,
   Ruler of the Universe

Teach us to listen
   to the silence posed by unanswerable
   questions
   to the silence imposed by the rupture of
   history
   and to that most frightening silence
   when we can no longer find you
   anywhere

Blessed art Thou O Lord our G-d,
Ruler of the Universe

Help us to remember
   when the memory is too distant
   and when the memory is too fresh
   when the memory is too painful
   and when the memory is too dull
   when the memory is too horrible
   and when the memory is too mundane
   and when we cannot remember,
   remember for us

Blessed art Thou O lord our G-d,
  Ruler of the Universe

Inspire us to act
  with extraordinary courage in the midst of ordinary times
  with ordinary goodness in the face of extraordinary crisis
  and with unbounded imagination that dares to risk the possibility of hope.

Teach us, help us, and inspire us
  to listen, to remember, and to act
  and never ever to quit. Amen.

Bruce Coriell

4

Invocation at A Memorial Service for A Trustee

O Lord our God, we ask your blessing as we gather in grateful memory of your servant Robert W. Woodruff. We offer to you our thanksgiving for his long and exemplary life, for all his contributions to the welfare of our city, and most especially, for his extraordinary confidence in Emory University. In remembrance of all his good works, renew in us the boldness of vision and generosity of spirit that value the common good above private satisfactions. So may this hour of recollection and gratitude be a fitting memorial indeed. Amen.

Donald G. Shockley

5

For a Music Faculty Member Who Led the Chapel Choir

God, who sustains our lives as we move from joy to sorrow,
  as we move from distress to thanksgiving,

> support us, each one, as we stand within this life-
> moment, today, now.

We are joyful to have touched and to have been touched by
  him whom we remember in our worship today;

> yet we are sorrowful that death has taken him from us.

We are distressed that he whom we knew as husband, father,
  family, as teacher, colleague, as artist, friend,

> we are distressed that he should die at this moment
> in life;

> yet we give thanks for having known a life that is
> measured best by its quality, not its duration.

Thus, within this life-moment, we pray not that our sorrow
  and distress be removed, but that they be transformed
  by our joy and thanksgiving.

God, continue to grant to the family and to each of us the gift of
  peace that passes our human understanding.

Above all, make firm within us and among us the conviction
    that the quality of our living will be better
    because we have known,
    because we have been touched by the life of Don Jones.

Amen.

Dennis W. Haas

6

At a Campus Service Following September 11, 2001

God of the ages,
we commend to you this night,
those lost to us for a while,
but always in your presence:
beloved sons and daughters,
beloved mothers and fathers,
beloved brothers and sisters,
beloved uncles, aunts and cousins,
fiancées, confidants, friends, companions.

We commend to you
the families whose tables now have empty chairs.
Comfort them in their sadness,
and grant them peace in their anger.
Let the love once shared
not be considered lost
but only redirected.

And, dear God, for all of us,
grant us your blessing in these dark days.
And may we hold on to the hard lessons we have learned:
that you made each individual by hand with love and care,
and that none is replaceable;
that the ties that bind us as community and nation
can never be taken for granted;
that our faiths must always be
defended against the perversions of hatred and violence;

that your justice, though it seems slow
and silent, is inevitable;
and that, on this earth, you are always with us,
because good people of all races and religions
show us the light of your presence
and the power of your truth.

Bless this university
this night,
that the trials of the last three weeks
might continue to draw us together
as a community of learning
and a family of friends.

So go forth in peace
in the loving spirit of those we have lost
honoring their legacy
and always remembering their joy in life. Amen

Ian Oliver

7

A Prayer to Conclude Memorial Services for Students

God, we have come before you with various thoughts and
 feelings:

  sorrow, loss, anger, bewilderment,
  gratitude, hope, trust, joy.

  We have been reminded again of our own mortality
  and of our possibilities.

God, we thank you for this time together and
 for the treasury of memories that will endure.

Help us to incorporate the best of our memories of (*name*)
into our living:

  that we may be more caring and sharing;
  that we may be more sensitive and loving in our living;
  that (*name*) may indeed live on in us and through us. Amen.

Dennis W. Haas

VIII. Prayers for Founders' Day Programs

1

Ethereal Mystery,
be praised in
a history of wisdom,
in vision become fruitful
in work and lives of the long rewarded,
giving and gracing our present.
Be gloried in those gone before.
Their faces now, we envision
framed in eternity's glow.

Ineffably True,
be lauded by hope and challenge,
ash and crocus, book, and instrument,
by life and work and future's vision.
Be honored
until future generations
remembering
rejoicing as we do now.

Eternal Joy and Delight
Be Always
in the music of sphere, string, and voice.
Amen.

Jan Fuller Carruthers

71

2

A Charter Day Dinner Invocation

Source of light and life, we give you thanks for Bishop John Henry Hobart and for all those whose vision for a college on the frontier resulted in this institution on the shores of Seneca Lake.

On this night of honor and of celebration we pray that Bishop Hobart's concern for inclusivity of race, religion and region may continue to be embodied in our ideals and practice;

that Hobart's desire to bring the revelations of contemporary culture to bear on tradition, even as he brought traditional understanding to bear on contemporary culture, might continue to keep us at the frontiers of intellectual and social advancement;

and that Hobart's method of reasonable dialogue might continue to be a path for discerning truths and building up community .

Fountain of action, we give you thanks also for those who have contributed to Hobart College for the past 176 years: for students and alumni, faculty and coaches, administrators and support staff, parents, friends and spouses; for all those who have committed their time, energy and passion to the mission of educating young men to be a positive moral force in the world.

Send your blessing on this gathering that we might honor and celebrate our history, even as we look to the future. Bless the food we are about to receive and the hands that prepared and serve it, that we might be strengthened to serve a hungry world. Amen.

Lesley Adams

3

Invocation for Heritage Day (Methodist) Convocation

Almighty God, all that we possess is from your loving hand. You have given us gifts which our forebears never dreamed of. For these we give you thanks and praise. We call to mind before you all those whom it would be easy to forget: the homeless, the destitute, the sick, the aged, and all who have none to care for them, and who have precious few resources.

Give us grace that we may honor you with all that we have and all that we are, especially by service to the least among us. Make us bold to follow the footsteps of blessed John Wesley, and all your followers who have given of themselves in remembrance of the forgotten on society's edge. In Jesus' name. Amen.

William McDonald

4

A Dinner Grace for Founder's Day

Holy and Eternal Friend,
we gather here and now
who are twice blessed.

Blessed we are in receiving the rich bounty of life
and its enjoyments:
breath to walk, life to think,
the belonging to Hollins which
enriches our souls with friends, laughter, and challenge.

Blessed again we are in giving back
to efforts which inspire not the duty, but the glad privilege
of upholding and sustaining the first and last gift.

So, Twice blessed by You,
we assemble to toast our double joy,
to feast and laugh,
to celebrate and commit ourselves to still great grace.
Be here, in presence, host and guest,
and hear us as we
give thanks,
and thanks again.

Jan Fuller Carruthers

5

Invocation for A Founders Day Luncheon

Creator God, another year has passed in the life and ministry of our covenanted community of faith: the Christian Church (Disciples of Christ) and Chapman University. As we look back on that year, we rejoice in the marvelous way your Spirit has moved among us, empowering us to make great strides in so many areas of campus life. For this we are truly grateful.

At this annual meeting we recall those men and women of faith whose spirit-inspired dreams and hard work gave birth to this institution. May we demonstrate that we are their spiritual heirs by responding to the Spirit's call to envision a bold future for Chapman University, and by committing ourselves to making a Chapman education available to students through generous contributions to the scholarship fund.

As we gather for this luncheon, we ask that you would bless the food to the nourishment of our bodies and the fellowship to the nourishment of our spirits. Amen.

Ronald L. Farmer

6

An Invocation for Founder's Day

Creative Spirit,
>be praised
>for beauty that sets our lives:
>green hills and shadowed valleys,
>sun-warmed meadows that stretch far with blessing.

Loving Spirit,
>be praised
>for the wisdom
>of Charles Lewis Cocke, our founder:
>in whose historic and living vision we still see,
>whose challenge yet invites us to justice
>and whose remembrance draws us again toward honor.

Powerful Spirit,
>be praised
>for the horizons of our souls:
>laughter and longing that will not be stilled,
>gratitude that pulses praise,
>awe that lifts our heads,
>and dreams that dance.

Be praised, Eternal Spirit,
in our pride and accomplishments
and in the power and hope of these gathered lives.
Amen.

Jan Fuller Carruthers

IX. PRAYERS AT OCCASIONS RELATED TO SPORTS

1

Two Invocations for an Athletics Banquet

Diving, stroking, running, kicking, lifting, throwing:
Let us celebrate the life of the body!

Strategizing, analyzing, critiquing, planning:
Let us celebrate the life of the mind!

Longing, competing, sorrowing, rejoicing:
Let us celebrate the life of the spirit!

Earth-maker, Pain-bearer, Life-giver,
we come together this evening to celebrate.

Soar with us in our celebrations,
that we might express fully our thanksgiving
for the coaches and team-mates, trainers and friends
whose encouragement and support give Herons their wings.

And at the end of the evening,
when the celebrations are over,
another year ended,
keep us mindful of your ever-present invitation to fly.

Bless now the food we are about to receive,
and the hands that prepared and serve it,
that we might find our bodies, minds and spirits
renewed for service to your world.

In the name of all that is Holy. Amen.

Lesley Adams

2

Holy One,

We give you thanks for the beauty of your creation:
> for flowers and fields, lakes and trees;
> for birds and all creatures which creep upon the earth.

We thank you for our bodies:
> for legs to walk and run and kick,
> for arms to throw and catch and stroke,
> for heads to observe, analyze, and strategize.

We thank you for hearts
> which enable us to form the bonds of friendship, team and community;
> and for the spirit which enlivens our bodies just as the air we breathe.

As we gather for this athletic banquet, we give particular thanks
> for those who have prepared the food which nurtures our bodies,
> for coaches and trainers who have coaxed the best from us,
> and for the student athletes whose spirit gives life to our community.

Be with us and bless us this night that we many be prompted to use our many gifts for the good of all creation and to your glory.

In your many names we pray. Amen.

Lesley Adams

3

Invocation for a Basketball Banquet

Our Father and Our God,

You have blessed us in ways we take for granted—with strength and ability, enthusiasm and agility. We do not presume to gather tonight to celebrate our own accomplishments. Many have gone before us. For those coaches, teachers, and players who have inspired us, we give you thanks.

For those who enable us to play this game—administrators, trainers, and janitors—we give you thanks.
For families who have encouraged us and made sacrifices; for those too numerous to mention who have had a part in this team, we give you thanks.

And, as we eat this meal, we remember that as this food sustains us, so it is with your Grace and daily Love. Amen.

Stewart Jackson

4

Dedication of a Women's Athletic Field

With joy and thanksgiving, O God, we gather to dedicate this athletic field to your honor and to the glory of sport. As Lord of life, we thank you for the pleasure derived from play; the self-confidence nurtured by competition; and the ecstasy experienced by both athletes and spectators.

Transform this land, eternal God, into a playing field in which the respect for rules and the spirit of sportsmanship abide. Imbue players and coaches alike with the knowledge that the most important goal is not the triumph but the struggle, not the victory, but the honor of representing our college.

Welcome all athletes, gracious God, who compete upon this turf. Be their constant companion in this place and in all the contests of life.

In the name of the one God, by whose love and grace we are all assured of eternal victory, we humbly pray. Amen.

Paul H. Jones

5

Invocation for an All Sports Banquet

O God, ever present and creator spirit, we come to this banquet in a spirit of thanksgiving and praise. We offer thanks for the opportunities to participate in sports and to serve others through teaching, mentoring, and coaching.

We praise and thank you for the gifts you have bestowed upon these student athletes. We thank you for their skills and talents and for the opportunity to compete and to grow through victory and defeat.

We offer thanks for dreams and visions to pursue, for challenges to embrace and for unforgettable experiences and close friendships with teammates and colleagues. We come acknowledging our gratefulness for coaches, administrators, trainers, sports medicine staff, faculty, friends and family for their support and encouragement, teaching and care.

Bless this gathering tonight as we honor accomplishments, hard work and dedicated effort by individuals and teams alike. Bless, as well, O Creator God, this food and the hands of the persons who prepared it for our consumption. With celebration and thanksgiving we pray. Amen.

K. James Davis

6

An Invocation for a Horse Show

Be praised O Creator by all your creatures
great and small
and in the beauty of your creation we see before us.
Be exalted in the wit and style and grace
of horse and rider,
in the elegance of the well-trained and the capable,
by the years of discipline demonstrated in this event.
May your heart be honored and glad,
O Mighty One,
as we gather;
and may your presence grace
us with courage, safety and fun for all:
riders, spectators, judges, and helping hands.
God's name be praised. Amen.

Jan Fuller Carruthers

7

Invocation for a Homecoming Football Game

Gracious God, in whose mind all good is imagined and from whose will all beneficent acts proceed, we thank you for this special weekend of reunion. We are grateful for the profound friendships and bonds to individuals and communities that shape our lives and draw us to homecomings. We acknowledge the privilege of having been part of the Millsaps College community and of higher education anywhere in this nation. Let us never take either experience for granted. As we move into this competition, we pray for the safety of both teams and of all who have traveled to this occasion. Bless this event and the schools represented. In the midst of the conflicts and challenges that face our community, society and world, enable us to make wise decisions and demonstrate healing behavior. Strengthen our commitment to the lasting values of diversity, equity, justice and truth so that we might bring hope to our world. For we pray in your spirit. Amen.

Don Fortenberry

8

Invocation for a National Tennis Tournament

O Lord, we are grateful on this day for all those things we often take for granted: for life and health, for strength of mind and body, for freedom to travel and to compete. We ask your blessing as we begin this national tennis tournament. May the experiences we have here, whether the disappointment of losing or the exhilaration of winning, give us new insight into ourselves and deeper appreciation for our dependence upon others. Finally, we ask your blessing on athletes everywhere in the world and pray that their dedication to competition based upon fairness may contribute to mutual understanding and peace. Amen.

Donald G. Shockley

X. Prayers for Alumni, Parents, and Homecoming Events

1

A Prayer on Alumni Weekend

God of all times, of all places, of all peoples:

On behalf of the alumni gathered here this weekend,

We give you thanks for a university
>   that provided them with a place
>   to begin to grow into the persons they now are
>   and have been throughout their adult lives.

We give you thanks for the faculty and staff
>   who challenged and supported them.

We give you thanks for the campus organizations
>   that provided them with opportunities to form relationships
>   that have lasted until today
>   and that are being renewed today.

On behalf of the university, we give you thanks for the alumni gathered here this weekend:

their achievements and contributions to the betterment of society remind us of why we are dedicated to higher education.

We give you thanks for their return to campus and the way it reminds the university of its history and of its influence. And we give you thanks for the ways they contribute to DePauw's ongoing work with young adults and commitment to future generations.

May the meals, gatherings, and activities this weekend overflow with the sentiments and joys that draw us closer to one another and closer to you. Amen.

O. Wesley Allen

2

Prayer for an Alumni Convocation

God, for the joy and celebration of this weekend,
    for happy memories of past days here, and
    for present sharing with old friends and new,

    we give thanks.

God, extend and deepen our gratitude:

    for the best of our yesterdays and the challenges of our
    tomorrows;

    for those whose love of wisdom, whose commitment
    to truth and beauty, to the development of mind and
    body, whose concern for us as persons has opened
    doors of new possibility for our lives;

    for successes to share and failures to learn from;

    for learning how to live with what is, without giving
    up on what ought to be.

God, extend and deepen our gratitude, then confirm within us
    and among us the prophet's mandate of old:

to do justice, and
        to love kindness, and
                to walk humbly with your God. Amen.

Dennis W. Haas

3

Invocation for an Alumni Luncheon

How good it is, O God, to be gathered in this place for this is an exciting weekend, a weekend when the past, the present, and the future hold hands! As alumni tell stories and share memories, we recall what Chapman was. As we attend the baccalaureate and commencement services we see what Chapman is. And as we see buildings under construction and hear of bold plans, we envision what Chapman will become. Yes, this is an exciting weekend, and we give thanks for the opportunity we have of participating in it.

As we gather for this luncheon, we ask that you would bless the food to the nourishment of our bodies, the program to the nourishment of our minds, and the fellowship to the nourishment of our spirits. Amen.

Ronald L. Farmer

4

At a Worship Service on Alumni Weekend

On this day, O God, we remember with thanksgiving those whose vision, commitment, and energy led to the founding of Emory University so many years ago. We give thanks for those in every generation who, as students, faculty, administrators, staff members, trustees, alumni and other friends, have sustained the life of the university in good times and bad.

Today we are especially grateful for those of our alumni who have returned to their alma mater for this weekend of memory and celebration. May their visit to this place renew in them and in us our commitment to the highest and best in the Emory tradition. We place before you today the names of the alumni who have died during the year. Accept our gratitude for their days among us and grant comfort and courage to all those most keenly affected by their passing. Amen.

Donald G. Shockley

5

Invocation at a Homecoming Football Game

Gracious God, creator of us all, we are grateful for this beautiful fall afternoon and for the nostalgia it evokes in us. As the passing of seasons reminds us of the movement of time, so does the passing of our days remind us of the precious nature of the gift of life. We thank you for the two fine institutions represented here and for that numberless stream of individuals—students, faculty, staff, parents, friends, supporters—who have sustained them and brought them to places of prominence.

On this special homecoming weekend, we acknowledge the contribution of dedicated and wonderfully competent faculty whose names ring in our memories with gratitude and affection; of staff who nurtured us and broadened our total educational experience; of parents who rejoiced in our triumphs and shared our pain; of peers who became friends; of the church out of whose bosom these colleges sprang; and of all those persons who have honored these institutions with their support and encouragement. Let us never forget that we are privileged people and that you ask us to use our privilege wisely and well.

We pray for the safety of players and travelers. As those who have been given much, we pray also for the energy and courage to seek vision without illusion, humility without dishonesty, passion without bigotry and gratitude without end, so that our heritages will be honored and the legacy of those who have gone before us will be enhanced. For we pray in and through your spirit and as your people. Amen.

Don Fortenberry

6

Invocation for a Parents' Day Breakfast

We praise you, O God, for all your goodness toward us. We are grateful that you have created the earth and made it both bountiful and beautiful. Your creation provides a feast for our eyes as well as food for our tables, making our hearts grateful and glad. Today we express our thanks most of all for our university and especially for our students and their parents. Unite us all in affection for this place, and in our hope for the full realization of its great potential for good. Amen.

Donald G. Shockley

7

A Prayer Given Each Year for the 50 Year Club

Compassionate and Holy God,

How do we celebrate an event that happens only after fifty years?
In a society obsessed with the future
    and forgetful of the past,
      how do we remember?

In a nation that counts nanoseconds and
    thinks a decade is forever,
      how do we measure time?

How do we celebrate an event that happens only after fifty years?

God of Israel, you charged your people
    to celebrate the Jubilee,
a year that came only once in fifty years,
a year to remember faithfulness
a year to take time
    time to correct past injustices
    time to heal old wounds,
    time to reaffirm commitments,
    time to rest,
    time to begin anew

God of Faithfulness and God of Hope
 make this day a Jubilee
 a day of joyful memories
 a day of hopeful beginnings. Amen.

Bruce Coriell

XI. Prayers for Faculty and Staff Gatherings

Four Prayers for Faculty Meetings

1

Source of all new life,
You know something of expectancy:
What will this new academic year be like?
>This new president?
>These new colleagues?

Creator of the universe,
You know something of labor pains and big bangs:
How will we make it through conversion to semesters?

Life Spirits,
You know something of dance:
Bless us with a lively balance
>as we weave our way through classes,
>>and advising,
>>>and meetings,
>>>>and our own creations.

Great Wisdom,
You know us:
Be with us in this coming year.
We will call on you many times.

Amen.

Lesley Adams

2

Lord, you have made us professors an odd lot. So varied are our fields, so complex are our views, so many are our tasks. Here together, in this place, we examine your creation and our own lives within it. What exhilarating, exhausting work! Your world is such a patchwork of wonder, and our disciplines, for all that they captivate us, barely grasp your imagination.

So, Lord, we pray, teach us humility and give us courage. Make us patient, but candid. Increase wisdom in us, and keep us teachable. Let our classrooms be windows, not on us, but on the wondrous world you have made, in which both you and we together take delight. Amen.

William McDonald

3

Timeless God, we gather once again to reconstitute our community
at the threshold of yet another year.

We assemble this afternoon both in gratitude and in need.
For the fresh insights and tireless energy of those who newly join us,
we are grateful. Grant that their scholarship and teaching will both
enlighten and enliven us and that their presence will renew our common life.

We pray, as always, for students: that they may discover in their
studies more delight than burden, more fulfillment than frustration.

But mostly, O God, this afternoon, we pray for ourselves and for our colleagues,
that our teaching may arise from impassioned inquiry coupled
with zest for living and care for those seeking to learn; and that our
relationships to each other and to our disciplines might be
marked by balance, health and wholeness.

Now, as we enter this new year, O God, temper our pride with gratitude for
the opportunities that are ours in this community.

Mend our brokenness. Knit tight the fabric of our common life, and grant us
wisdom that nurtures common good and transcends individual interests.

We offer this prayer in your name, author of us all. Amen.

William Finnin

4

Let us pray:

Gracious God, we trust that we are collected here for good purpose, that with all our differences we share a common intent: to welcome an equally diverse student population and to entrust to them matters that are sacred to us. We share what we have learned, and we learn what they have to share.

May it be our good fortune this year to enjoy our differences, to embrace them as gifts and not permit them to segregate us: faculty from groundskeepers or maintenance or administrative staff. Save us from hierarchies of self-importance. Give us the grace to believe that everyone here is a treasured part of the family, that all of us, in some manner, are teachers. And that whatever is dysfunctional in this family is not powerful enough to undo the good that we are here to do.

In this world that You have made, Life is not static. We are players on a moving stage. And we have the grand privilege of taking part in the formation and transformation of lives. It is sacred work that we do. Bring us every day, in every encounter with colleagues and with students, to the awareness that we share with one another the nourishment of memory, of Elon's strong traditions. And we are here to see our mission unfold in the lives of students, as their encouragers, coaches, and mentors.

Nothing this precious can be accomplished without struggle, but that is the vocation to which we are called and for which we are being prepared by Thy grace. Amen.

Richard McBride

5

Invocation for A Judaic Studies Convocation

O, God, you who are known by many names, we pause before you to give thanks for this meal and for those who prepared it for us. We eat this meal in secure surroundings, in good health, with friends, and with the pleasant expectation of hearing from our distinguished guest. But we are not so self secure that we have forgotten that most of the world does not share our fortune. So with the rumblings of war on a distant horizon, we pause not only to ask your blessing, but to ask for the courage to live, and pray, and to work for peace in the world. God of many names, guide us in this work for your names' sake. Amen.

Stewart Jackson

6

For a Faculty and Staff Dinner at the Beginning of a New Year

Gracious God,

We praise you for your many gifts:
For the gift of language, with which we fashion poetry and discourse;
For the gift of sound, on whose wings soar melody and song;
For the gift of intellect, with which we probe the mysteries of atom and cosmos, the world you have made and the lives you have given us.

Bless all who make teaching and learning possible in this place, and prosper their efforts.

Bless our food and conversation this evening, and move our hearts to gratitude, that with hearts joyful and true, we may raise to you lives that radiate your creative glory. And let your people say, AMEN.

Mark Radecke

7

For a Faculty and Staff Holiday Party

God of many names who is beyond all names,

We gather to celebrate together as we draw close to the end of the semester. Many here are preparing for Christmas or Chanukah, or are observing Ramadan. We ask that people of all faiths and those of none can find a place of welcome here at Agnes Scott College, that we might continue to be a community which values the free exchange of ideas and the search for truth.

We give thanks for all the hard work and achievements of this semester: for teaching and learning in the classrooms and in the city; for buildings nearing completion; for programs and relationships which have nurtured the individual and corporate lives of our students, faculty and staff. Most of all, we give thanks for the people who made these achievements possible, for those who give their all to make Agnes Scott what it is.

May our time together for this meal and celebration strengthen our love and trust in one another. We give thanks for the food that we are about to receive, for the hands that prepared it, and for all good gifts in our lives.

I pray in the name of the One for whom a star shone, and who was sheltered from the cold in his mother's tender arms. Amen.

Laura S. Sugg

XII. Prayers for a Variety of Occasions

1

A School of Nursing Pinning Ceremony

God, whose love has brought healing since the beginning of time,
we gather to honor another generation of nursing graduates at this institution.

May knowledge and compassion pour out of these accomplished students to sustain the miracle of life through their informed attention and concerned commitment, easing the personal wounds and physical strife that hinder humankind.

Array all who are pinned in a grace so radiant that it glimmers in each of their eyes, and illuminates hope in all who receive their care,
making this moment not simply a twinkling star in the lives of new nurses, but a brilliant beam of light in the endless spectrum of healing.

Ashley M. Cook

2

Invocation for a Girl Scouts Gala

Holy, Mighty, Tender One
Blessed, blessed be!

When they say we are unequal,
we remember our awesome creator.

When some call us imperfect,
we assert your Holy Name.

When we feel less than beautiful
we wrap around us your deliverance.

When it seems we cannot
You remind us that nothing is impossible.

Now do continue to bless us with your Presence,
with Peace, Justice, Understanding;
With striving, growing, and simple trust.

When we celebrate success
we ask You, be our Guest and Host,
the light of our community.
When we eat, be our nourishment and our love.

And as we are, and will be,
we bid you, take always delight. Amen.

Jan Fuller Carruthers

3

A Prayer on Moving Up Day

God of roots and wings,
we give you thanks for the fertile places in our lives
and especially for William Smith College.

> Planted here, we have found nourishing soil and taken root;
> and, whether in spite of adverse conditions,
> or because of good pruning,
> we have grown and perhaps blossomed.

Ground of our Being, Object of our highest desires,
we give you thanks also for the unexplored vistas of our futures.

As we come to the end of this ritual acknowledgement
of the pain and promise of transition,
We hear your call to "come up a little higher!"

Give us, we pray, as we move upward and onward,
the capacity to stay grounded even as we fly. Amen.

Lesley Adams

4

In a Residence Hall on Friday Night

It's finally quiet. Too quiet. Roommates have gone home for the weekend. Or on dates. Or to the movies. Or to a game. The quiet would bring some peace with it, if we who are huddled here were not so lonely and a little bored. But, Lord of crowds and solitude, Lord of great flocks and a few sheep, we who are here can rejoice together in your presence. You are here. We are not alone. Lord, visit with us this night. Craft these hours into an encounter with you and with each other that bears fruit in a new community of friends, a new way of caring for one another, of bearing one another's burdens, and sharing of one another's joys. Thank you for this unlikely, but extraordinary, evening. In the name of Jesus, our friend. Amen.

William McDonald

Two Prayers in Celebration of the Martin Luther King, Jr. Holiday

5

God of love,
We gather here today to remember a man who answered your call to speak and to act on behalf of your loving justice. This man also spoke of shattered dreams, and the hard, hard work of nonviolent direct action. Inspire us today to follow Dr. Martin Luther King Jr.'s example as voices for the voiceless, as ones who choose love over hate, even at great cost.

Give us the strength to love. At times it can feel as if we can't make a difference. Help us to know deep inside our frightened hearts that, with you beside us, we can change the world.

Dr. King spoke of the beloved community. I pray that the community of Agnes Scott College can draw ever closer to being a place where every person—student, faculty or staff member—is empowered and loved and respected, not in spite of his or her difference, but because of it.

Prevent us from believing the lie that evil is dead. Open our eyes to our own hatreds, our own prejudices, so that we can speak and act out of love and not fear.

Thank you for this day and for the life and witness of Dr. Martin Luther King. We are thankful for all people who work with little earthly reward to make this world more like the one about which he dreamed.

Facing the rising sun, of our new day begun,
Let us march on, till victory is won. Amen.

Laura S. Sugg

6

Our creator god, we pray that you bless our gathering here tonight as we come to remember your beloved servant, the Reverend Dr. Martin Luther King, Jr. Bless us as we remember his life, as we honor his ministry and witness, and as we celebrate his dream.

Help us this night and always to remember that Dr. King's witness came from his commitment to serve you as a minister of the gospel of Jesus Christ. Help us to remember his call to us to live with love and compassion, to right wrongs, to seek justice for all brothers and sisters, and to create peace among all persons.

On this night on which we honor Dr. King, it is right that we offer our prayers for peace throughout the nation and throughout the world. Hear our prayers for those who struggle today against a rising tide of racism and hatred, joblessness and poverty, homelessness and hunger.

Let us seek to follow the example of Dr. King by being ambassadors of hope and peace, seekers of justice here and everywhere, and by being those who convey to others a presence of love and compassion.

Bless this gathering, bless our music, and bless the words and thoughts of our speaker, that Dr. King may be honored well and that you, O God, may be made known to us both this night and in our living of each day to come. Amen.

K. James Davis

7

A Prayer at the Inauguration of a College President

Holy Spirit of all power, truth, and grace,
> high above all, yet deep within all of us,
> we gather to ask your blessing on this college
> and especially our new President.

Inspire in her person your likeness:
> innocent strength, exuberant joy
> deep, attentive listening,
> persistent caring and tough beauty.

May she be known for:
> the scope of her agile mind,
> the vision that commands and calls her,
> the lives she touches across years of fruitful service.

Also move, we ask, in the hearts of all
who offer themselves as members of this community.
> Thrust us into kindness of which we think we are not able.
> Tempt us into braveries that appear impossible.
> Nudge us into commitments that seem now unimaginable.

O Eternal Glory,
be lifted up in the eyes and life and work of your beloved daughter Janet.
And may this day stand as the threshold of blessing—
rained down, sloshed around, poured out, shining and elusively hopeful—
for teachers, learners, workers, and players
who sojourn here in this Your blue green valley.
May it be so. Amen.

Jan Fuller Carruthers

8

A Christmas Prayer

On that holy night,
Somehow,
It happened.

Somehow,
God took a handful of humanity:
Proud, petulant, passionate;
And a handful of divinity:
Undivided, inexpressible, incomprehensible:
And enclosed them in one small body.

Somehow, the all too human
Touched the divine,
And was not vaporized.
To be human was never the same,
But forever thereafter,
Carried a hint of its close encounter with the perfect.
And forever thereafter,
God was never the same,
But carried a hint of the passion of the mortal.

If God can lie down in a cattle-trough,
Is any object safe from transformation?
If peasant girls can be mothers to God,
Is any life safe from the invasion of the eternal?

If all this could happen, O God,
What places of darkness on our earth,
Are pregnant with light waiting to be born this night?

If all this could happen, O God,
Then you could be, and are, anywhere, everywhere,
Waiting to be born this night in the most unbelievable places,
Perhaps even in our own hearts. Amen.

Ian Oliver

9

Following a Sermon on Human Sexuality

God, there's so much talk about sex: some good, some not;
some meaningful and helpful, some foolish and degrading.

Deliver us from ignorance and confusion in our talking and
thinking and acting.

Deliver us from bondage to a narrow morality that stifles
human growth.

Deliver us from a false freedom that would enslave and
harm others.

God, give us true freedom:

free our minds to discern that which is indeed beautiful,
true and good in all our relationships with other
persons;

free our voices to speak openly, honestly, and thoughtfully
about our sexuality in an atmosphere of mutual concern for
personhood; and

free our lives from the constant temptation to use
persons and love things, whereas our greater challenge
is rather to love persons and use things.

Mighty God, who in love created male and female, declaring,
"It is very good!" reveal to us that goodness intended for
us and guide us in the pursuit and enjoyment of that
good in the spirit of love and integrity and thanksgiving,
in the spirit of Jesus. Amen.

Dennis W. Haas

10

Invocation for AIDS Awareness Week

We gather, O God, as people of faith
> to remember those who have died from this terrible disease,
> to express our love and compassion for those who are suffering,
> and to pledge ourselves anew to work for the elimination of AIDS
> through education and medical research.

We ask that you would
> bless those who suffer physically and emotionally,
> sustain those who care for the ill and who comfort the grieving,
> and grant wisdom and perseverance to those who search
> for better treatments and vaccines.

Enfold us all in your loving arms, O God. Amen.

Ronald L. Farmer

XIII. A Selection of Benedictions

1

Following the Inauguration of a University President

Our Creator God, source of wisdom, compassion and understanding, we ask for your blessing as we depart from this celebration of the inauguration of our university's new president. As we affirm your presence in our midst, we dare to step forward with confidence and conviction as the University of Puget Sound prepares to enter the next century.

We ask for your blessing and continued presence as we chart our course for the future. May the course be one with a vision for how best to develop your gifts to us of the mind and of the heart so that those who leave these halls of learning may go forth with a clear call to serve our community, our nation and our world.

We pray that you place your blessing upon Susan Resneck Parr as the new president of the University of Puget Sound. As we offer thanks for the gifts which you have bestowed upon her and which she brings to this community of teaching and learning, we ask that you give her strength and vision, tenacity and patience, conviction and compassion. Bless and sustain her through the joys, rigors and challenges of her position, that she and the university may successfully seek the fulfillment of our mission together.

Bless, we pray, this University of Puget Sound; bless its faculty and staff; bless its students and their families; bless its alumni and alumnae; bless those who serve as its trustees. Bless all those gathered here today that we may go forth in joy and thanksgiving. Amen!

K. James Davis

Benedictions for Baccalaureate Services and Commencement Programs

2

benediction: to speak well of

Go now and

May passion inspire you
May injustice trouble you
May hope comfort you

May children teach you
May parents indwell you
May mountains join you
May angels protect you

May you sometimes get it right
May you laugh when you don't

May love surround you
May peace permeate you
May gratitude overwhelm you

Go now
   knowing that good and loving
   words have been spoken
   for you, and

May you always hear the call of spirit.
   Amen

Bruce Coriell

5

As you go from this place to use your education and your gifts in service to God's world, may the road you travel rise up to greet you, and may the wind be at your back.

And if your road refuses to rise up, follow it boldly into the valley for God is in the valley. And if the road rises high and becomes steep, follow it to the summit of the mountain, for God is on the mountain. And if you feel the wind in your face, stretch out your wings and fly on the Spirit's promise that God will never leave you or forsake you.

So now go in peace, with your face shining like the sun; and boldly follow your path into the future wherever God may lead you. Amen!

Vernon LaSala

6

Each beginning demands an ending
Every ending promises a beginning
    Now is such a time

Every meeting awaits a leaving
Each leaving remembers a meeting
    Here is such place

Now is as good a time as any
Here is as fine a place as you will find
    Go now and commence

Bruce Coriell

7

Benediction for a Medical School Commencement

You have been acknowledged one by one; you have been honored; and you have taken your oath. The years of anxiety and hard work have reached an important milestone. Other hurdles will arise before you; the challenges will never be done. But now is the moment to take satisfaction in all that has been mastered and achieved. Now is the moment to send you on your way with words of blessing.

Let me borrow them from the Native American lexicon:

> Oh our Mother the Earth,
> Oh our Father the Sky,
> Weave for us a garment of brightness.
>
> May the warp be the white light of morning,
> May the weft be the red light of evening,
> May the fringes be the falling rain,
> May the border be the standing rainbow.
> May you walk fittingly where birds sing
> And where the grasses are green.
>
> In beauty it is done.
> In harmony, it is written.
> In beauty and harmony, it shall be finished.

And let us all say, Amen.

Rabbi Susan Laemmle

XIV. Two Prayers for Chaplains Themselves

1

For the 50th Anniversary of the National Association of College and University Chaplains (NACUC)

We who are guests
Bless the host!

And praise You for
the wisdom of these gathered souls,
for the families, communities,
and centers of learning they represent.

We praise You
for NACUC,
for friendship, support,
professional family and training,
for our small progresses toward
being as open-hearted as You.

Be praised for the rich lives
of those who once were present with us
who have gone before us,
who by their marks on us
are still present in us,
moving us forward into blessing.

Now be praised
by our celebration,
by laughter and blessing,
wine and bread,
as we joy in what is
and accept the challenge of what is to be.

We who are guests
Bless the host. Amen.

Jan Fuller Carruthers

2

At a Banquet of the Association for the Coordination of University Religious Affairs (ACURA)

Fount of Wisdom, Source of all truth,
Our God of many names:

We live in a beautiful, but broken world,
one that in this moment cries out for us to hear Your voice.

God of mercy and mystery,
Tonight we gather at these tables of plenty as humble, grateful people
who have come together searching for sustenance to nurture and strengthen us
so that we may bring light and healing to our communities.

And we have found it.
We have found it in the eyes, minds, hearts and hands of one another these last two days
and we are so very grateful.

We stand before you energized and fortified
by the unmistakable truth of Your love,
made real through suffering and celebration.

God of all generations,
You dwell in a light unapproachable,
often beyond the power of our thoughts to comprehend
and yet it is our most cherished life's work to try.

Enable each of us to be a new kind of contemplative;
challenge us to not close our eyes to find You
but to bravely keep them wide open in the chaos and the pain
so that we may look deeply into Your aching world.

Most gracious God,

We ask you, draw us closer to a new realm of trust and hope;
let us envision a time when sorrow and suffering are no more,
where violence is extinct and human flourishing is in abundance,
where the chains of ignorance, hopelessness, hate, and fear will no longer bind
us.

Sailing silently among the stars this evening, hear our prayers, embrace
our hearts, and gird our souls.

And for this we say, AMEN.

Sharon M. K. Kugler

Contributors

Lesley M. Adams was ordained to the priesthood in the Episcopal Church in 1988, and has been Chaplain at Hobart and William Smith Colleges in Geneva, New York since 1995. Prior to her current appointment, she was the dean of students at Colgate Rochester Divinity School/Bexley Hall.

O. Wesley Allen, Jr. currently teaches homiletics at Drew University in the Theological School and the Caspersen School of Graduate Studies, in Madison, New Jersey. From 1996-2002, he worked in campus ministry at the Wesley Foundation at Georgia Tech, then served as dean of the chapel at DePauw University, in Greencastle, Indiana.

The Reverend Dr. Jan Fuller Carruthers is in her 16th year of ministry as Camp Younts Chaplain and Assistant Professor of Religious Studies at Hollins University in Roanoke, Virginia. She formerly served as Baptist campus minister at Yale University. Raised in Beirut, Lebanon, she has now spent half her life in the United States.

The Reverend Ashley M. Cook is Chaplain and Director of Church Relations at Piedmont College in Demorest, Georgia. A minister in the National Association of Congregational Christian Churches, she served as pastor of churches in Pennsylvania, Oregon, and Connecticut before assuming her position at Piedmont College in 1999.

Bruce R. Coriell serves as chaplain of Colorado College, following stints at Vanderbilt University and DePauw University. Whenever he thinks he is starting to get the hang of public prayer in the academy, someone asks him to offer one of his "non-religious prayers." He lives in Colorado Springs, Colorado, when he is not off wandering the rivers and mountains.

K. James Davis is currently completing his 26th year as Chaplain at the University of Puget Sound in Tacoma, Washington, having previously served as Director of the Wesley Foundation and Campus Minister for the United Campus Ministry at the University of Minnesota in Duluth. He is active with his wife, Nancy Tam Davis, in work devoted to personal and global change through dialogue and discernment.

Ronald L. Farmer has served as Dean of the Wallace All Faiths Chapel and Associate Professor of Religious Studies at Chapman University in Orange, California, since 1997. An active member of the Society of Biblical Literature and the Center for Process Studies, Dr. Farmer has written two books and numerous articles in the fields of biblical studies, hermeneutics, and interreligious dialogue.

William Finnin has served as University Chaplain at Southern Methodist University in Dallas, Texas since 1980. Prior to that time, he was for eight years the inaugural director of The Uniting Campus Ministry at Louisiana State University in Baton Rouge. He served two terms as president of the Association for the Coordination of University Religious Affairs. He edited a book, *The Morality of Scarcity*, published by LSU Press.

Donald P. Fortenberry has served as chaplain at Millsaps College in Jackson, Mississippi, for nearly three decades. The quality of his work was recognized when the United Methodist Foundation for Christian Higher Education selected him to be Chaplain of the Year in 1995. His work on campus is strongly mission-oriented, enabling students, faculty and staff to participate in many community service organizations, such as Habitat for Humanity and Hospice Ministries.

Dennis W. Haas served as chaplain of Grinnell College in Grinnell, Iowa, from 1966 to 1996. He continues to serve the college in a half-time appointment as Professor of Religious Studies. His prayers included in this volume are from his book, *To the God of Many Names.*

Patricia Hunt has been chaplain to Mary Baldwin College in Staunton, Virginia, since 1985. She serves as a member of the Religion Department faculty and directs the Quest Program, a unique concept that helps students integrate religious commitment, intellectual development and service. From 1976-1985 she served local church pastorates in West Virginia and Tennessee.

Dr. Stewart A. Jackson, Dean of the Chapel at Birmingham-Southern College in Birmingham, Alabama, served as Chaplain of the College for 21 years prior to his present role. International service learning projects have been a distinctive feature of his ministry for many years. In 2000, he accepted additional responsibility as a Marriage and Family therapist for the United Methodist Board of Pastoral Care and Counseling serving Alabama and West Florida.

Paul H. Jones, an ordained minister of the Christian Church (Disciples of Christ), is a member of the faculty at Transylvania University in Lexington, Kentucky. Prior to his full-time teaching assignment, he served as Dean of the Chapel and Professor of Religion at Transylvania.

Rabbi Susan Laemmle, Ph.D has served as Dean of Religious Life at the University of Southern California, in Los Angeles, since 1996. Prior to her appointment as Dean, she served as Director of the Hillel Jewish Center at USC. Rabbi Laemmle's academic background is in English Literature, and she often uses literature, particularly poetry, in liturgical settings.

Vernon F. Lasala is Chaplain of Ohio Northern University in Ada, Ohio. Prior to his present appointment, he served pastorates in the East and West Ohio Conferences of The United Methodist Church. He currently serves on the executive committee of the National Association of College and University Chaplains in his capacity as treasurer of the organization.

Kerry Ann Maloney has served as Chaplain to Bates College in Lewiston, Maine, since 1996. Prior to that time, she served on the chaplaincy staff at Boston College for twelve years. Her areas of special interest include the integration of contemplative spirituality and social activism, the impact of religious pluralism on contemporary spiritual life, literature and the religious imagination, and women's theologies and spiritual development.

Richard W. McBride, a minister in the United Church of Christ, has been University Chaplain at Elon University in Elon, North Carolina for the last eighteen years. With the exception of his years as a student at Union Theological Seminary in New York City, Rev. McBride has lived his entire life in the eastern foothills of the Appalachian Mountains of Virginia and North Carolina. He has also served in campus ministry at Wake Forest University and Gardner Webb University.

William P. McDonald is College Pastor and Assistant Professor of Religion at Tennessee Wesleyan College in Athens, Tennessee. He holds the Master of Theological Studies degree from Duke University Divinity School and a Ph.D in the History of Christian Thought from Vanderbilt University. Earlier in his career he served as pastor to United Methodist and Lutheran congregations.

Reverend Linda J. Morgan-Clement has been the Henry Jefferson Copeland Campus Minister at the College of Wooster in Wooster, Ohio, since 1996. Prior to that time, she served for eight years as an Associate Synod Executive in the Presbyterian Synod of the Northeast. Earlier, she served two congregations in the Presbytery of Milwaukee, Wisconsin. In addition to her ministry at Wooster, she chairs the board of directors for Montreat Conference Center in North Carolina.

Ian Oliver serves as University Chaplain at Bucknell University in Lewisburg, Pennsylvania. Previously, he was Associate Chaplain at Kodaikanal International School in South India, and served as Assistant to the Dean of the Chapel at Kalamazoo College in Michigan. He presently serves on the executive committee of the National Association of College and University Chaplains.

The Reverend Susan K. Olson has served as chaplain to Wesley College in Dover, Delaware, since 1999. Prior to her service at Wesley, she served as the first Helen Carnell Eden Chaplain to Wilson College, in Chambersburg, Pennsylvania, for six years. She is ordained in the Presbyterian Church, USA.

Mark Wm. Radecke was appointed to the chaplaincy of Susquehanna University in Selinsgrove, Pennsylvania, a college of the Evangelical Lutheran Church in America in 1997, following eighteen years of parish ministry in southwest Virginia. A graduate of the Lutheran Theological Seminary in Gettysburg, he is currently pursuing doctoral studies at Princeton Theological Seminary. Three volumes of his sermons have been published.

Donald G. Shockley retired in 1999 after a long career as a university chaplain, having served at Birmingham-Southern College, in Alabama; the University of Redlands in California; and Emory University in Atlanta, Georgia. The author of a book, *Campus Ministry: The Church Beyond Itself*, he now lives in Brentwood, Tennessee, where he remains active as a writer, editor and consultant for ministries in higher education.

Laura S. Sugg is chaplain and assistant professor of religion at Agnes Scott College in Decatur, Georgia. She formerly held similar positions at Davis and Elkins College in West Virginia, and Hanover College in Indiana. She also served as Presbyterian campus minister at James Madison University in Virginia. She earned a Ph.D. in theology form the University of Edinburgh, Scotland, and is now writing a book on Celtic Christianity.

Gay H. Welch is University Chaplain at Vanderbilt University in Nashville, Tennessee. She holds a Ph.D. in Ethics and, as assistant professor in the Department of Religious Studies, teaches courses in feminist theology and ethics. She has four children, two grandchildren and three dogs.

D. Darrell Woomer, Ph.D. an ordained minister in The United Methodist Church, is Chaplain of Lebanon Valley College in Annville, Pennsylvania. He has served as pastor of churches in eastern Ohio and is also a certified Minister of Music.

0-595-26579-0